✛ An Observer's Guide

Making Clothes—Stage 1

Cutting Out

Toni Naldrett

Illustrations by Barbara Firth

FREDERICK WARNE

Published by Frederick Warne (Publishers) Ltd, London, 1982
©Frederick Warne (Publishers) Ltd, 1982

Imperial and metric measurements are used throughout the book.
Choose either the metric or imperial system and stick to it throughout
each project—changing from one system to the other will lead to
inaccuracy and mistakes.

ISBN 0 7232 2892 2

Filmset and printed in Great Britain
by BAS Printers Limited, Over Wallop, Hampshire

Contents

Introduction

It can be said of any creative project undertaken, from cooking a meal, or decorating a room to making a dress, that the final product reflects the amount of thought and preparation given at the beginning. This book is a guide to the thought and preparation needed for dressmaking. It will help you make the best choice of design in commercial paper patterns or magazine offers, and to find the right size for you. Advice is given on choosing suitable fabrics and making wise buys. It shows you easy ways of measuring yourself, altering your pattern to fit you and preparing to cut out your fabric. Finally there is a section on how to mark your cut out garment before beginning to sew on your machine. Do try to follow these planned phases of work—a simple, organized pattern of preparation will help you to make successful clothes.

Above all relax and enjoy your sewing knowing that your hobby will give you creative satisfaction, individual fashion appeal and save you money!

For help in further steps in dressmaking—using your sewing machine and fitting and pressing your garments—look for other titles in this series.

Before you start

Equipment

There are a few pieces of equipment for preparing paper patterns and cutting out which you are strongly advised to acquire. Any expense incurred at the outset will be more than recouped by the professional finish your clothes will have as a result.

Adhesive tape   For repairing tears or cutting mistakes in paper patterns. They need instant mending as they are very fragile.

Pencils   A lead pencil and blue and red crayons are basic requirements for altering your patterns.

Pins   Buy the longest, finest pins you can find. These are sometimes called 'long and fine' or 'lace' pins.

Shears   Good quality, long-bladed scissors are necessary to achieve a clean and even stroke when cutting fabric.

Tacking thread   Save all left-over reels of thread for this job. You can even re-use a length of thread again and again.

Tailor's chalk   This is used for marking instructions on fabric and can be brushed off afterwards. It is available in either cake form or as a pencil.

Tape measure   In view of the confusion over metrication of measurement, a tape with both imperial and metric markings is best.

Tracing wheel and paper   This small serrated wheel is used with carbon tracing paper for speedy transference of pattern markings on to fabric.

Yard or metre stick　　This is not essential but it does help in all dressmaking processes.

These are yours! Don't let the family borrow them.

Where to work

It is a good idea to find an organized place to work that suits you and to keep this for your dressmaking.

1　You will find that to concentrate all your equipment in one place will save time and energy. Many home-ideas magazines have articles on organizing space-saving work places. If space and finance are limited, a large pin-board made from thick cork tiles or ceiling board mounted on the wall will give space to hang equipment, and pin paper patterns and inspirational fashion pictures. This will also create a pleasant, organized corner in which to relax and enjoy your sewing.

2　A good working light, either natural or electric, is necessary. This will eliminate fatigue and eye strain when sewing and help in colour matching of notions and fabrics.

3　A flat, smooth surface is really essential to lay out fabric and patterns successfully. A clear stretch of floor is frequently better than the dining-room table. There must be sufficient space to lay out the fabric in one piece if possible, otherwise confusion and mistakes can arise. Do as much preparatory work as possible, on the paper pattern and fabric, at a table surface at a comfortable work height for you, but take to the floor to lay out and cut the fabric. If your knees protest at the prospect of crawling about to cut out your wardrobe, how about a sheet of hardboard, 1×2 m (3×6 ft), laid on top of your table surface? This sheet could also double as a suitable pressing table top and can be stored under a bed or behind a door. Alternatively, a paper-hanger's folding table is another inexpensive and easily-stored method of providing a good cutting table.

Phase 1

Important choices—pattern, fabric and body measurement

Your choice of pattern

With your first ventures in making clothes, don't make the mistake of thinking that the smaller the garment the easier and quicker it will be to make. A simple dress with no fastenings, made up in a stretch knit fabric will be more fun to do and certainly more successful.

Before you purchase a commercial pattern or make up a magazine pattern gather as much information about the chosen design as you can.

1 Know your own body. A regular and honest assessment of your figure, hair style and make-up will help in the choice of the right design and rejuvenate your ideas on styles for your wardrobe. Time and fashion move on—it's fun to keep up with them and not be left behind with a dull appearance.

2 Will the design you have chosen complement your existing wardrobe? Do you require new blouses or sweaters to wear with it? All these facts add up to more time and money and considering them could save wasted effort on your part.

3 Does the pattern give good value for money? Many designs include co-ordinated separates to make with the basic design. These packages give excellent value financially and make good fashion sense.

4 Read the written description of the garments illustrated. This will tell you the details that are perhaps not visible, such as the kind of fastenings to be used and whether the garment should be lined. Are you confident enough to undertake the dressmaking techniques required for these details?

9

Your choice of fabric

Choosing fabrics is one of the most enjoyable aspects of dressmaking. A myriad of colour and textural sensations await you. But it can be difficult, if you are a beginner at dressmaking, to visualize the lovely picture of your chosen design into the reality of the right fabric. Again, more information is needed.

1 Pattern companies and magazines will provide a list of suggested and unsuitable fabrics for the design. All the designs offered to you are exhaustively tested in a variety of fabrics before being marketed. The weight, stretchability and appearance of the material are all vital to the success of your chosen design. If the pattern company says that obvious diagonal, patterned or woven fabrics are not suitable, take their expert advice and choose something suggested. The names of some of the fabrics may be unfamiliar, so ask the store assistant for guidance.

2 Handle the fabric before you buy it. Draping a length over your arm will give you a good idea of its weight and how it will hang.

3 To test for 'nap', smooth the fabric out with the palm of the hand. If the surface pile brushes to and fro and changes colour you might need extra fabric. Similarly, if the fabric has a one-way design, consult the pattern envelope for yardages for material with nap.

4 Take the roll to an alternative light source. Colours change with different light conditions.

5 The fabric table on the back of the pattern envelope will tell you how much fabric each design will need. There are three standard widths of fabric, so first find the width of your chosen fabric, then follow across the column to your pattern size to establish the amount of material to buy.

The table will look something like this:

	12	14
90 cm (36 in)	2.40 m ($2\frac{2}{3}$ yards)	2.40 m ($2\frac{2}{3}$ yards)
115 cm (45 in)	2.20 m ($2\frac{3}{8}$ yards)	2.30 m ($2\frac{1}{2}$ yards)
150 cm (60 in)	1.30 m ($1\frac{1}{2}$ yards)	1.30 m ($1\frac{1}{2}$ yards)

For instance, a dress in size 14 will need 2.30 m, or 2½ yards, of fabric 115 cm (45 in) wide.

6 When you buy your material note any special washing or dry cleaning instructions.

Body measurement

I cannot stress strongly enough how important accurate body measurements are to the dressmaker. Measurements are best taken wearing your underclothes or at the most a lightweight dress. Note each measurement in imperial and metric figures on the chart provided (p. 43). Keep the chart safely as you will need it each time you begin a new pattern.

Always run the tape measure over your bust, waist and hips each time you begin to sew a garment—just in case!

To take accurate measurements follow the chart and Figure 1.

1 *Bust* This must be measured in a straight line around the body, across the nipples in the front. Don't allow the tape to droop across the back. Breathe naturally and measure comfortably close to the body.

2 *Waist* It helps to put on a belt to define your natural waistline. Take this measurement underneath the belt. Don't cheat and pull it too tight—you'll suffer later.

3 *Hips* The hip line should lie about 23 cm (9 in) below the natural waistline, using the bottom of the belt to establish your natural waistline. Measure in a straight line around the body, comfortably close, as with the bust measurement.

4 *Bust point* This is one of the most important measurements to take for pattern alteration, to ensure a good fit to your garment. Pretend you are wearing a dress that has a round, collarless neckline. Place the tape at the point where the neck and shoulder seams meet and measure down to the point of the nipple. Before doing this adjust your bra straps as they loosen in the wash. You will be surprised what a tonic to your figure raising your breasts can be.

5 *Front neck to waist* Measure from the same point at the neck as in **4**, but follow over the nipple to the natural waistline, the bottom edge of your belt.

6 *Front neck to hem* Measure as in **5** but continue to the skirt length you like to wear.

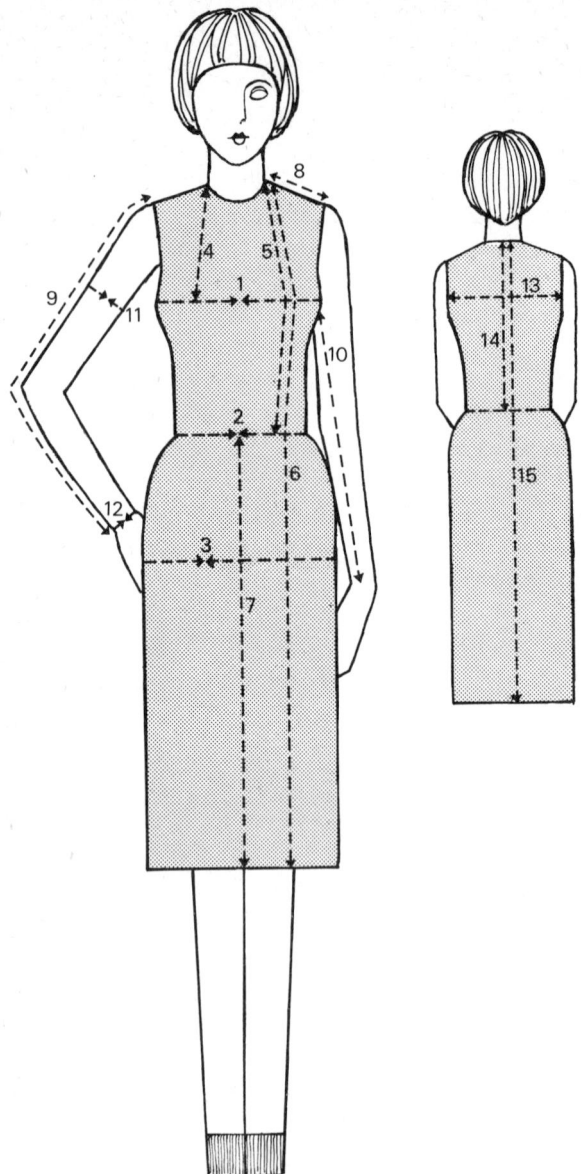

Figure 1

7 *Front waist to hem* This is a special skirt measurement. Start from the natural waistline, the bottom edge of your belt, and measure down to the desired hem length for your skirt.

8 *Shoulder* This is another important measurement for good garment fit. Start at the same point as in **4** and lay the tape along the shoulder to the top of the shoulder bone.

9 *Upper arm* This measurement is taken with your hand on your hip. Start from the top of the shoulder bone where measurement **8** ended and lay the tape along the top of the *bent* arm, over the elbow, to the wrist bone.

10 *Under arm* Place the tape measure up into the arm pit and continue down underneath the *straight* arm to the wrist bone.

11 *Top arm* Having established the sleeve length you now need the upper and lower arm circumference to ensure a good fit. Measure round the plumpest part of your arm—again not too tight!

12 *Wrist* This measurement is taken closely round the wrist bone. This will give you the minimum circumference needed for a tight sleeve with zip or button opening. For straight sleeves with no opening establish the minimum circumference required by measuring around the closed fist.

Turn around now and continue to follow the chart and back-view illustration. You will find a friend's assistance is necessary here.

13 *Across back* Clasp your arms across your body to hunch your upper back. This gives the widest spread you will need to make your garment comfortable. Explain to your helper about the imaginary dress in measurement **4** and ask her to measure you, about 10cm (4 in) down from the top of your neck, from one imaginary sleeveless armhole seam across your hunched back to the other invisible seam line.

14 *Back neck to waist* Measure from the small prominent bone at the base of the neck down to the natural waistline—bottom of the belt again. This measurement will be shorter than **5** because your bust is not in the way!

15 *Back neck to hem* Continue down from natural waistline to desired hem length to match **6**.

Which pattern size for you?

All paper patterns are cut to standard sizes. Commercial pattern catalogues and magazine pattern offers have size charts for you to find your correct size. Many pattern companies also produce patterns cut for different height and figure proportions. For example, if your bust measurement is 87 cm (34 in) but height and figure proportions are shorter than average, 'half-size' patterns would fit you better than those in the 'misses' or 'womens' categories.

It is wisest to choose all coat, dress and suit patterns according to your bust size, in spite of differing waist and hip measurements. You will find that most of the complications of fit and style occur around the upper part of the body. If adjustment is needed, it is simpler to do it in the skirt area. So, for example, if your bust measurement is 87 cm (34 in) or 89 cm (35 in) use pattern size 12. However, if you want to make a skirt or trousers, use a pattern for your hip measurement.

Bargain buys

There is especial pleasure in buying fabric unexpectedly, without a specific project in mind. That bargain price or beautiful length you cannot resist. There is a quick method of calculating approximately how much fabric you will need, designed to help you make 'wise buys' when purchasing remnants of fabric without a specific design or commercial pattern in mind. This method applies to simple designs. Flared panels, checks and obvious one-way patterns need more fabric than these basic lengths.

All you need to know to use this method, for any garment, is the length of the main pattern piece on you. How long would a dress or skirt be? If the design will have sleeves, how long will they be? Add this information together in the following way to find the approximate length you require.

As a basic rule you will need twice the main pattern pieces plus hem allowance on narrow 90 cm (36 in) fabric. Normal sleeves are narrow enough to fit into the folded fabric and be cut once. On wider width material the main pattern pieces will fit in side by side on the folded fabric, unless your hips are wider than 140 cm (54 in) or 150 cm (60 in) width fabric. If this is the case the main pieces must be laid on the fabric as though for 90 cm (36 in) width. Using

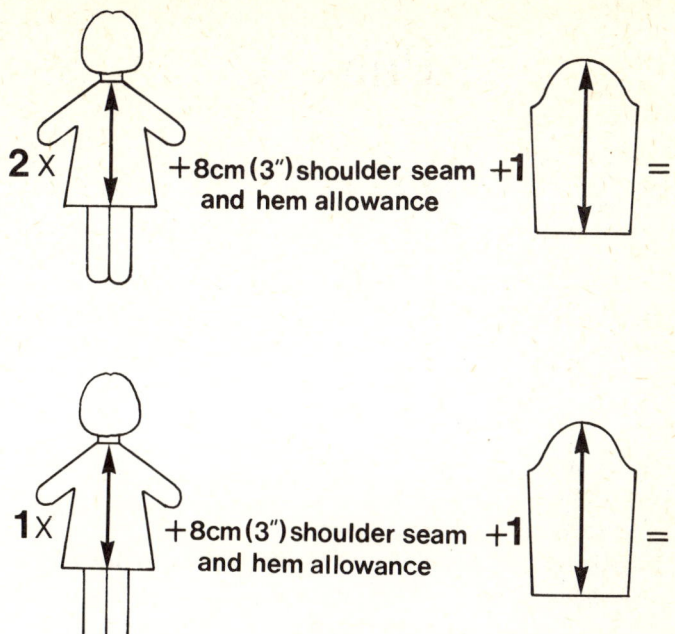

2 × +8cm (3") shoulder seam **+1** =
and hem allowance

1 × +8cm (3") shoulder seam **+1** =
and hem allowance

Figure 2

the measurements you have just taken, calculate as shown in Figure 2.

As an example, for a long-sleeved dress that measures 112 cm (44 in) from shoulder to hem and has 46 cm (18 in) length sleeves, the calculation for 90 cm (36 in) and wide material would be as follows:

2 × (112 cm + 8 cm) + 46 cm = 286 cm, or 2.86 m *or*
2 × (44 in + 3 in) + 18 in = 112 in, or $3\frac{1}{8}$ yards

The calculation for the same dress in 150 cm (60 in) wide material would be:
112 cm + 8 cm + 46 cm = 166cm, or 1.66 m *or*
44 in + 3 in + 18 in = 65 in, or $1\frac{3}{4}$ yards

Turn to the back of the book and note down all the measurements given there. Cut out the page and carry it in your purse. You need never waste money on the wrong length again!

15

Phase 2

Preparing your pattern

Fitting the pattern to you

Paper patterns are made to standard sizes—we are not. The final perfect fit depends on figure posture and the hang of the fabric. It is obviously not possible to accommodate all figure problems in this first fitting process but the basic length and circumference alterations can be made on the paper pattern. This will save time in the unpicking of the half-made garment to make corrections and so avoid possible over-handling of the fabric which results in a dish-rag dress.

To alter your paper pattern to fit your figure you will need your own body measurements that you have taken and the measurements your chosen design will make up to. When the two sets of measurements are compared you will be able to see which areas require alteration. To find the FINISHED size of your pattern measure from STITCHING line to STITCHING line, or STITCHING line to FOLD line, down the length and across the width of the pattern as in Figure 3. Use the figure measurements chart for guidance on where to place the tape.

To MEASURE AND ADJUST LENGTH

Front and back neck to waist (**5** & **14** on chart)   Always measure and alter this before checking and correcting the overall neck to hem length. See Figure 4 for methods of alteration.

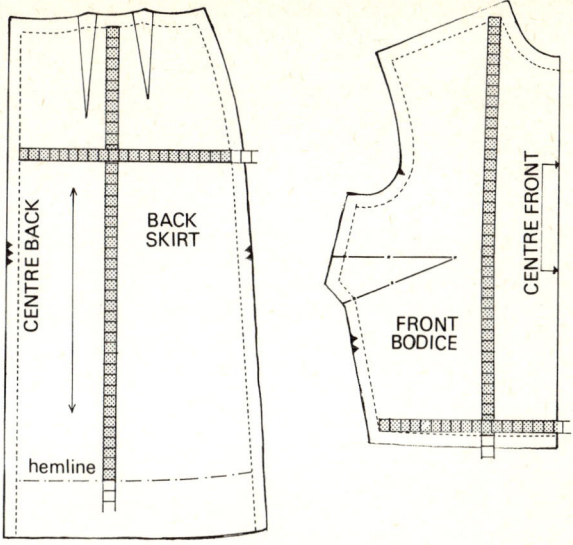

Figure 3

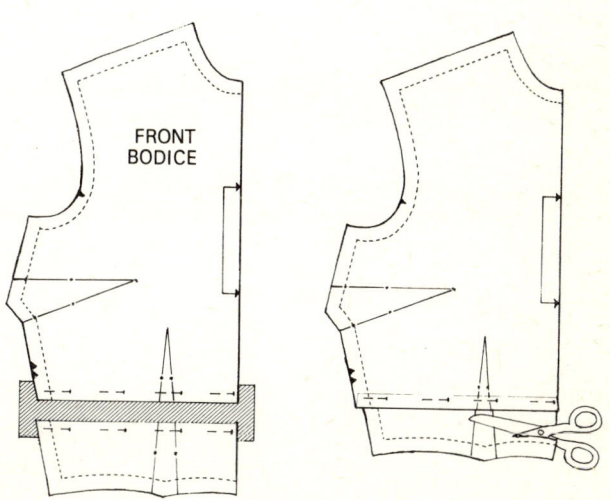

Figure 4

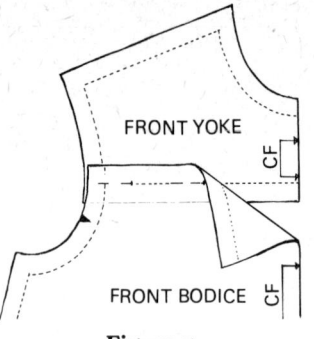

FRONT YOKE

CF

FRONT BODICE   CF

Figure 5

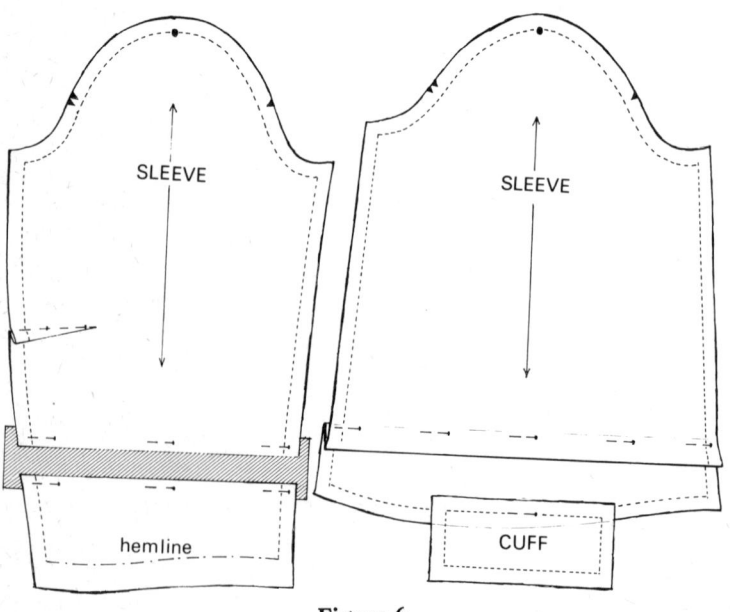

SLEEVE

SLEEVE

hemline

CUFF

Figure 6

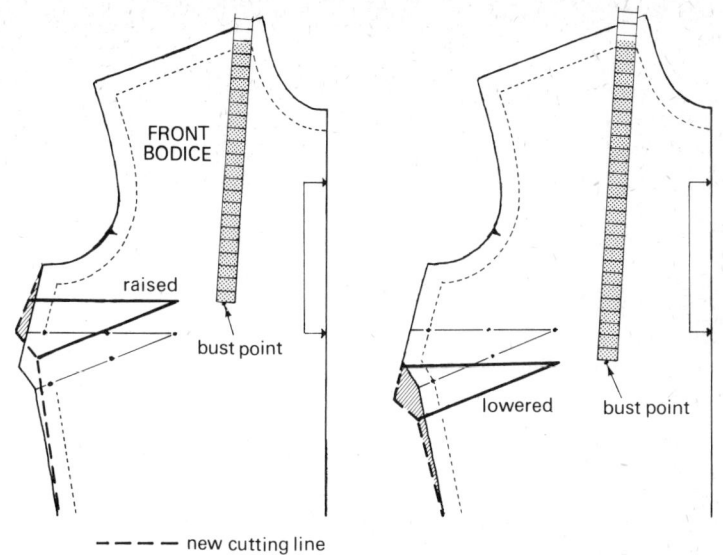

FRONT BODICE

raised

bust point

lowered   bust point

— — — — new cutting line

Figure 7

Front and back neck to hem (**6** & **15**)   Measure from base of neck to marked hem line. If you have a design with a waist seam or yoke across the body, pin the pattern pieces together as in Figure 5, stitching line on top of stitching line, then measure for the finished length. Alter facing lengths to match for jackets and coats.

Sleeve (**10**)   Remember to assemble the complete sleeve, ie pin on cuff pattern pieces, or pin the elbow dart closed, before you measure for the final length. See Figure 6 for methods.

Bust point (**4**)   The bust dart should finish approximately 4 cm (1½ in) to the side of the nipple. This measurement will show if the angle of the dart is correct for your bust. See Figure 7 for alteration methods.

19

If you had adjusted or graded (the technical term) your pattern to your exact measurements, the finished garment would be as tight as a second skin. To allow you to get in and out of the garment and be comfortable while wearing it, you must add EASE, see Figure 8a. The amount of ease will vary from design to design and you must judge how much is needed. The *minimum* ease that should be added is 2.5 cm (1 in) to the bust, waist and hips. This would give a very close fit. The more flare there is to your design, the more ease you will need to add to your basic measurements. Always check the finished circumference on the pattern (see later instructions). You may prefer less fullness, particularly at the hem, and could save fabric by reducing it.

All adjustments should be done equally, otherwise you will end up with a lop-sided garment. So the amount you wish to add or subtract must be divided equally between the four side seams, as shown in Figure 8b.

Bust, waist and hips (**1, 2** & **3**) Measure as before from stitching line to stitching line, or stitching line to fold line, across the body of your pattern, at the same points at which you measured yourself.

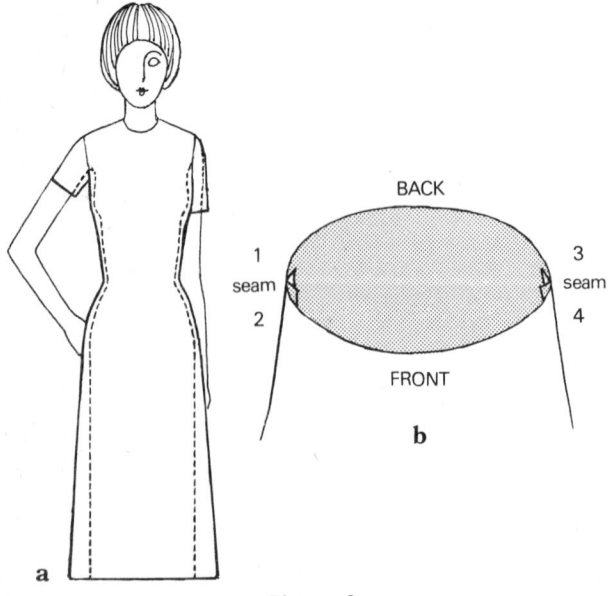

Figure 8

20

When measuring to find the finished size of the bust, waist and hips remember that the pattern represents only half the garment, so DOUBLE the measurement to get the complete finished size. Remember to close all darts that lie in the path of your tape. (See Figure 9 for quick method). Compare these with your own figure measurement, to which you should have added the amount of ease

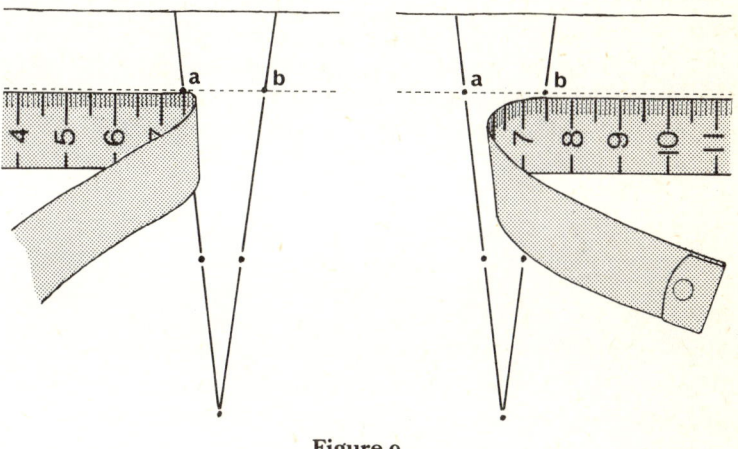

Figure 9

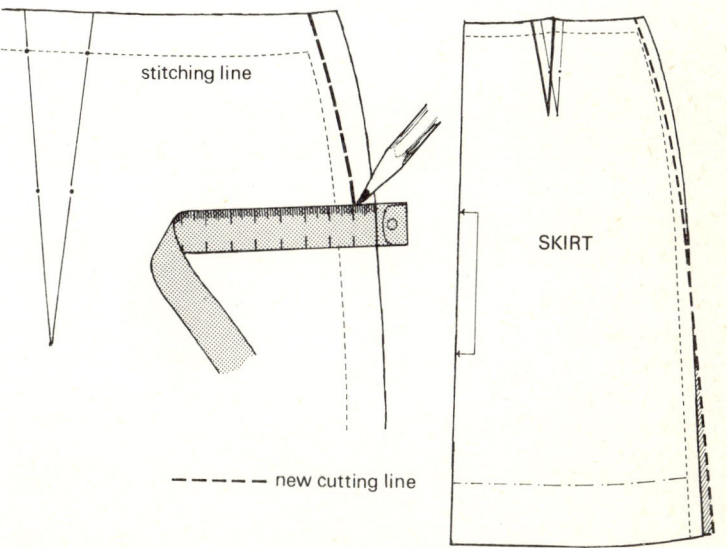

Figure 10

21

you feel that the style requires. Finally divide the difference by four and add or subtract that amount from the *outer cutting edge* of the pattern and redraw the cutting line down the side seams—BACK and FRONT! Move all darts in or out by the same amount to keep the balance of the style (see Figure 10).

Sleeve—upper arm (**11**)   There are several important points to consider should you wish to change a sleeve pattern. Always remember when adusting the width of the upper arm sleeve that the armhole on the bodice pattern must be altered to fit the new circumference of the sleeve. Measure from stitching line to stitching line for the finished width. Compare this to your personal measurement to which you should have added ease—a tight, fitted sleeve requires about 2.5 cm (1 in) ease—and divide the difference by two. (There are only two sides to a sleeve not four as in the body of the garment.) Now add or subtract the answer from the cutting edge, as in Figure 11. If, when adjusting the upper sleeve, the head of the sleeve is altered in any way then the armhole of the body pattern must be changed to fit, by adding or subtracting the same amount at the body side seam under the armhole.

If you have difficulty matching the sleeve head pattern to the armhole pattern, try comparing the two as illustrated in Figure 12. This is a useful way of finding out whether you can transfer one sleeve pattern to another body style. Pin the shoulder seams as shown. Start by matching the underarm seams exactly and roll the sleeve round the armhole, matching each set of notches. It is important that the underarm curves from the side seam to the first back and front balance notches should match. These can be let in or out as shown in Figure 11. The surplus on the sleeve pattern between the two balance notches and the head of sleeve mark is usually between 4 cm (1½ in) and 5 cm (2 in). This allows for the gathered ease on the finished sleeve head which will be eased into the armhole. However, should the surplus measure more than 5 cm (2 in) it will be difficult to ease into the armhole other than in pleats.

Sleeve—wrist (**12**)   Repeat the process as above and draw in the new cutting line from the underarm to the wrist.

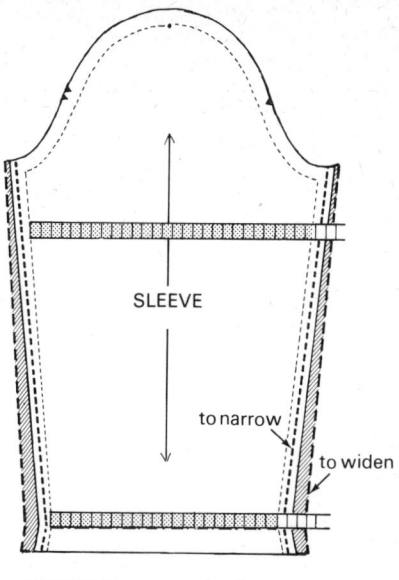

SLEEVE

to narrow

to widen

‑ ‑ ‑ ‑ ‑ new cutting line

Figure 11

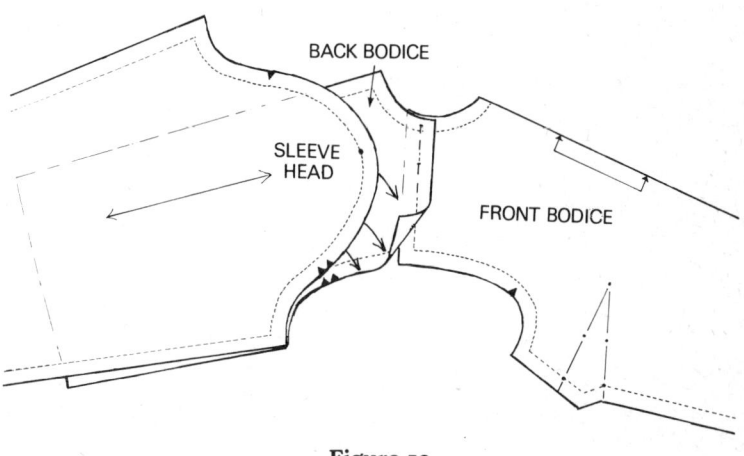

BACK BODICE

SLEEVE
HEAD

FRONT BODICE

Figure 12

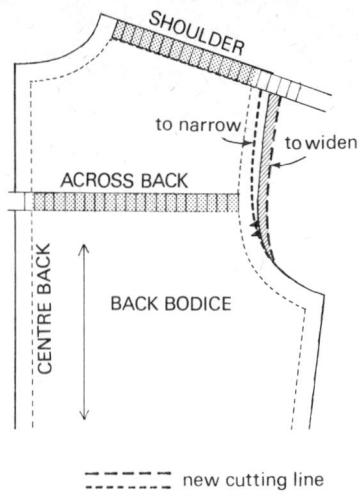

---- new cutting line

Figure 13

To MEASURE AND ADJUST ACROSS BACK AND SHOULDERS

Across back (**13**)   Measure across the back of your pattern from armhole seam line to centre back line or seam line. Remember to double this measurement and then compare it to your own. If there is any difference, divide this by two. (There are only two sides to your back, not four as in the body of your garment.)

Shoulder line (**8**)   Measure from the neck seam line to the shoulder seam. Subtract or add the difference between this and your own shoulder measurement at the armhole end of the shoulder cutting line, as in Figure 13.

Pattern alteration—a step-by-step programme

To sum up then, here is a programme to follow when altering a paper pattern.

1   Recheck your body measurements. It will improve the final fit of your garment to measure over the correct bra and girdle for your chosen design.

2   Roughly cut out the pattern pieces from the surrounding paper. Leave enough spare paper around the pattern to enlarge your pattern if necessary. Keep some extra paper and adhesive tape to hand to help here.

3   Pack away unwanted pieces, it saves confusion.

24

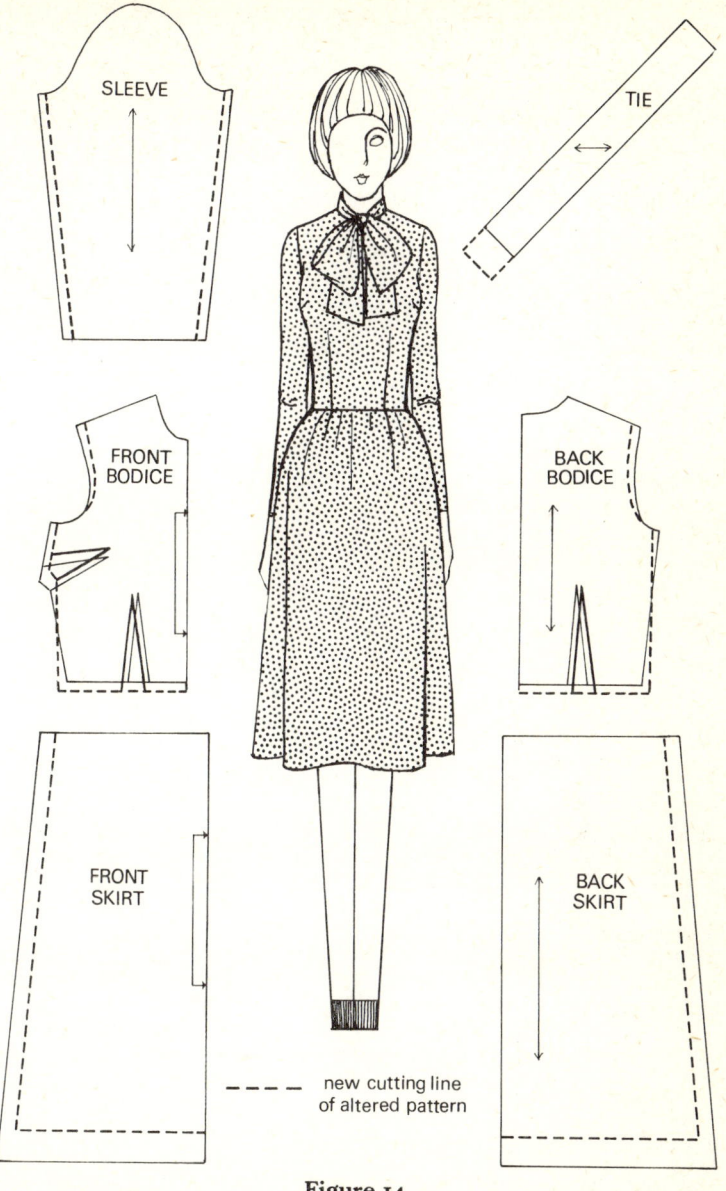

SLEEVE

TIE

FRONT
BODICE

BACK
BODICE

FRONT
SKIRT

BACK
SKIRT

– – – – new cutting line
of altered pattern

Figure 14

Pattern pieces for the dress illustrated. Dotted lines show the alterations
calculated on the chart on page 26.

Chart comparing finished pattern size with actual body measurements

Measurement	Finished pattern size		Self		Alteration	
	cm	in	cm	in	cm	in
front neck to waist	43	17	46	18	+3	+1
back neck to waist	41	$16\frac{1}{4}$	43	17	+2	$+\frac{3}{4}$
front neck to hem	116.5	46	111.5	44	−5	−2 (add 5 cm (2 in) hem allowance)
back neck to hem	114	45	109	43	−5	−2 (add 5 cm (2 in) hem allowance)
underarm sleeve	44.5	$17\frac{1}{2}$	44.5	$17\frac{1}{2}$	—	—
bust point	25.5	10	23	9	2.5	1 (raise)
bust	91	36	86 + $\underline{2.5}$ = 88.5	34 + $\underline{1}$ = 35 ease	−2.5 − 1 (÷4)	(−0.6 −$\frac{1}{4}$ each side)
waist	68.5	27	71 + $\underline{2.5}$ = 7.5	28 + $\underline{1}$ = 29 ease	+5 + 2 (÷4)	(+1.25 +$\frac{1}{2}$ each side)
hips	165	65	94 + $\underline{46}$ = 140	37 + $\underline{18}$ = 55 ease	−25 −10 (÷4)	(−6.25 −$2\frac{1}{2}$ each side)
upper arm	32	$12\frac{1}{2}$	32	$12\frac{1}{2}$	—	—
wrist	26.5	$10\frac{1}{2}$	21.5	$8\frac{1}{2}$	−5 −2 (÷2)	(−2.5 −1 each side)
across back	37	$14\frac{1}{2}$	35.5	14	−1.5 − $\frac{1}{2}$ (÷2)	(−0.75 −$\frac{1}{4}$ each side)
shoulder line	14	$5\frac{1}{2}$	11.5	$4\frac{1}{2}$	−2.5 −1 (each side)	
length of tie	63.5	25	76	30	+12.5	+5

4 Iron pattern pieces if necessary.

5 Measure pattern pieces to establish finished pattern size. Remember to follow the layout of previous examples for trouble-free working.

6 Complete any necessary alterations. Use a red pencil for the new stitching line and a blue one to indicate the new cutting line.

7 Trim round the new pattern shape.

8 CHECK: Are *all* the pattern pieces correctly altered, back and front and matching little bits?

9 Clear away scrap paper and tidy cutting area before starting to work with your fabric.

Quick tip

No more torn or tattered favourite patterns! Gently press paper pattern pieces onto lightweight fusible interfacing with a warm iron.

Combining patterns

It is often difficult to find the exact pattern design that you want. The body might be right but the sleeves or the collar are wrong! Perhaps you want to change details on a favourite basic pattern shape? This kind of simple pattern adaptation can be undertaken when you have been sewing for a while. The following are some ideas to make this task simpler together with some techniques for creating new styles from old.

1 Never throw away a pattern after using it—some detail may be useful later.

2 Collect your patterns into a pattern library. Dressmaking friends, clubs and classes can contribute and share in this bonus. It will increase the range of designs you can choose from in an economical way.

3 If you cannot find the design you have in mind in the pattern catalogues, search for the closest general body shape and alter it to your own satisfaction.

4 Alternatively, look through the shirt and blouse section of the catalogue, as often the correct design for the top half of the garment can be found here. It is easy to lengthen the pattern to your needs by following the instructions on page 34.

5 Have a good mirror handy to check the new pattern shapes pinned together on yourself as you go along.

6 Adapt your pattern AFTER you have completed the necessary figure alterations.

7 Always remember to add seam allowances to your new necklines, seams and alterations if necessary.

Adapting patterns

The cut and open technique is one of the basic methods used in pattern cutting to alter the shape of your pattern. Be careful not to use it on patterns made for 'stretch knit' fabrics. It can be used in the following ways, on all other patterns.

To MOVE BUST DARTS (Figure 15)

Decide where you wish the new dart to lie and draw, then cut through, this new line on your pattern piece. Fold and pin the original dart to close it and the new dart will open. Do remember that for a flattering shape the bust dart should finish 4 cm (1½ in) to the side of the nipple.

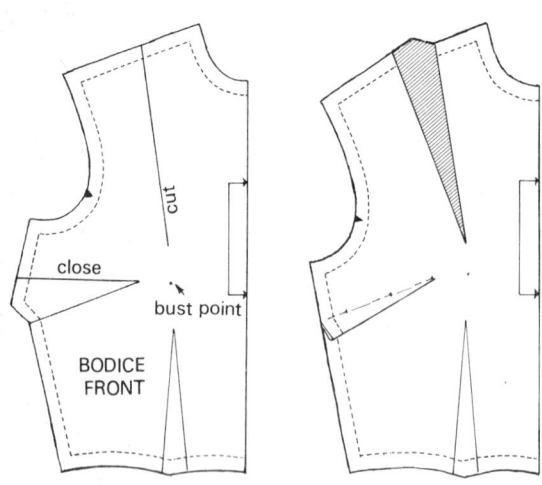

Figure 15

To increase fullness in the body (Figure 16)

This should be attempted with care as it is easy to overdo the fullness and end up with a tent rather than a dress. One way to avoid this is to use a yoke on your new design. The neck and shoulder area is close fitting to appear slimming while the body can be concealed gracefully in soft folds. Follow the illustration for the method. REMEMBER to include seam allowances and to repeat what you have done on the back of the pattern for a balanced effect.

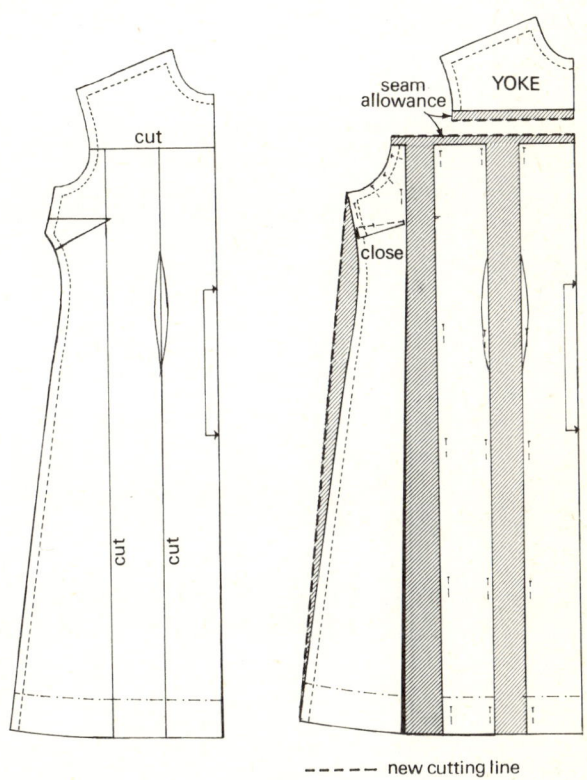

– – – – – new cutting line

Figure 16

To make a flared skirt (Figure 17)

By using the slash and dart closing technique you can add flare to a straight skirt. It may, of course, be sufficient for an A-line shape to draw in the extra width to the side seam—method 1 in Figure 17. For extra flare and swinging movement in the skirt, slash up to the base of a waistline dart, close the dart and extra flare will appear. Pin or tape the slash to tissue paper to hold its position. Finally round off the hem line to complete the new pattern (method 2).

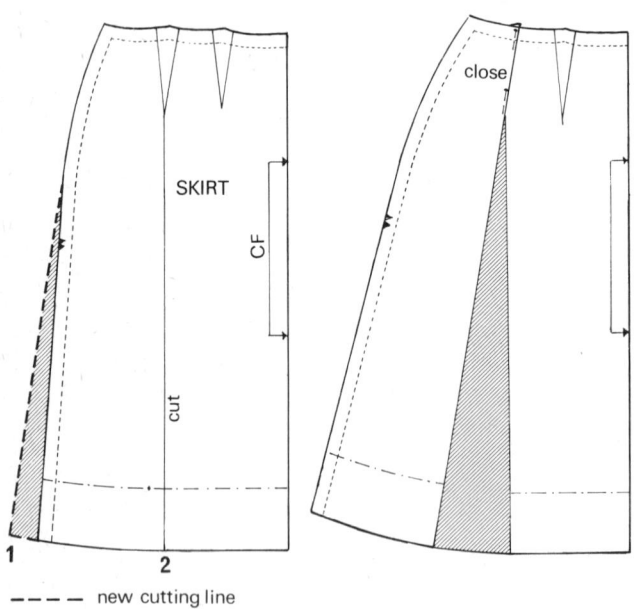

- - - - new cutting line

Figure 17

To INCREASE FULLNESS IN THE SLEEVE (Figure 18)

Decide on the length of sleeve you require. This method can be used for short puffed sleeves and long, generous bell sleeves. Cut away the surplus pattern—after the hem allowance has been added! Now slash the pattern as illustrated to just below the sleeve head and spread the sleeve to the desired fullness. Finish the pattern as for the flared skirt. The fullness in the sleeve can be left to swing or be contained by a cuff or a simple hem with elastic threaded through.

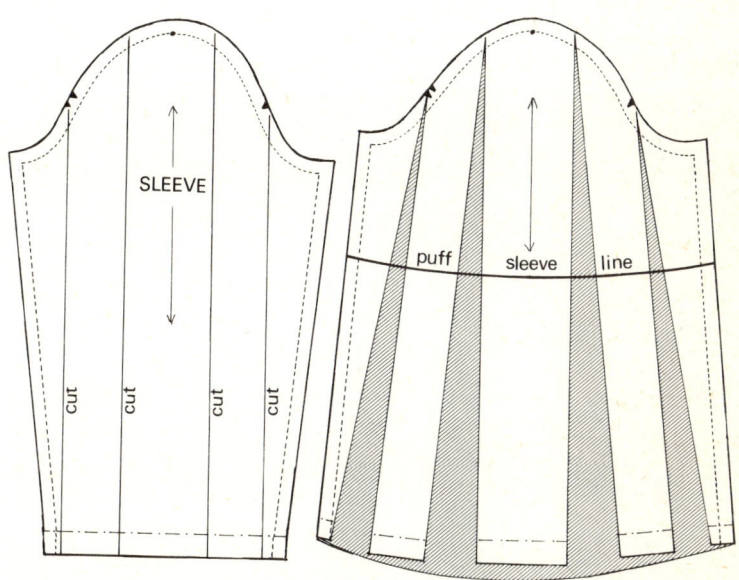

Figure 18

To CHANGE A NECKLINE (Figure 19)

To change the neckline of your pattern, lay the front and back body pieces together as illustrated. This will ensure that your new neckline follows through from back to front in a pleasing line. Add seam allowances and recut new facings on another layer of tissue.

This pattern layout will help you gauge whether a collar from another design will fit your neckline. Lay the collar around the neckline, carefully matching back centre fold or seam and shoulder notches. It is then easy to see where any adjustment will be needed.

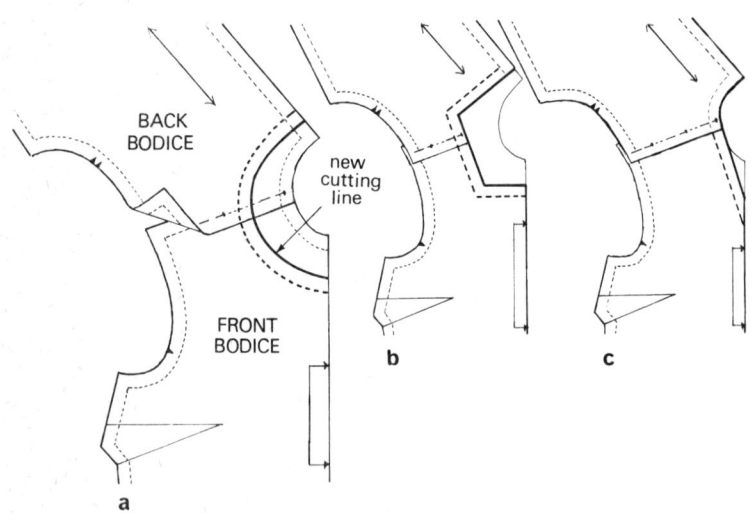

Figure 19

To make openings for button fastenings (Figure 20)

One way of adding a button-through opening to a favourite dress or blouse style is to pin or tape extra tissue under the centre front or back line and mark a line 3 cm ($1\frac{1}{4}$ in) from the centre along the length of opening you need.

There are two ways to make a facing for this extension. A separate facing is made by adding an extra seam allowance on to the edge of this new line and tracing around the whole outer edge of the neck and opening on to a fresh piece of tissue. Figure 20 shows the method for making an all-in-one facing with the button extension. Measurements to remember are 3 cm ($1\frac{1}{4}$ in) for a blouse or dress opening and 4.5 cm ($1\frac{3}{4}$ in) for a jacket or coat. If you plan to use larger than normal buttons on your garment, increase the button space accordingly.

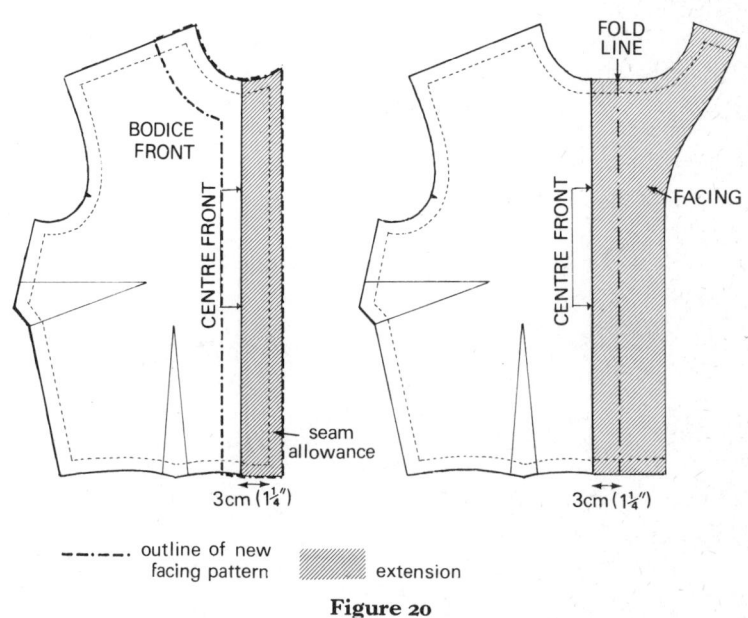

— .— . outline of new facing pattern   ▨ extension

Figure 20

To LENGTHEN A BLOUSE PATTERN TO MAKE A DRESS (Figure 21)

Pin or tape your blouse pattern on to a large piece of tissue and continue the front and back lines down the tissue. You will also need to draw a line across the tissue, 23 cm (9 in) down from the waistline, to show the hip level. Having measured from your waistline down to the length you would like your garment, mark this measurement on to the tissue, measuring from the waistline printed on the pattern, and add a hem allowance. Using the same method as for hip-line adjustment on page 21 calculate your hip measurement plus design ease and divide by four. Mark this on to the hip-line and then draw a new cutting line between the end of the pattern and the new hem line. You will often find the blouse pattern is long and wide enough to fit over your hips. In this case you can simply extend it as described to a new hemline.

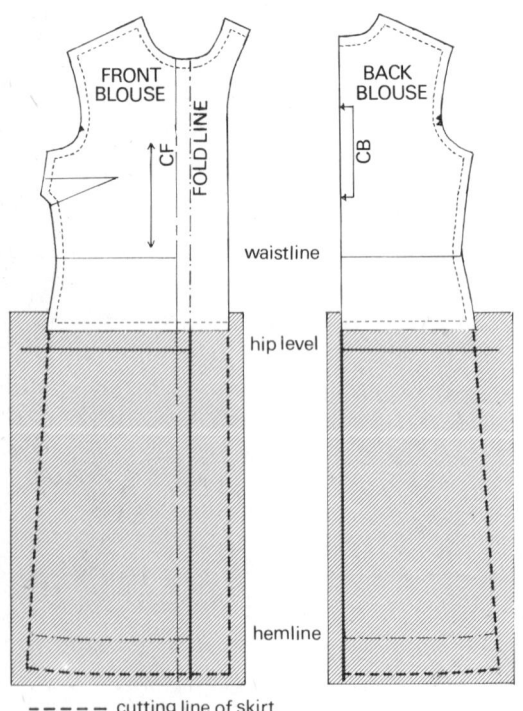

Figure 21

34

To make a dolman sleeve (Figure 22)

This adaptation can only be done with a pattern for set-in sleeves and preferably using a design without darts near the underarm area. First of all decide on the width, length and depth of curve you need for this dolman sleeve. Attach the front bodice pattern to a large piece of tissue and position the front underarm seam point of the bodice and sleeve as shown. Proceed as illustrated. The 5 cm (2 in) gusset curve in the illustration is the minimum amount required for ease of movement. Repeat the process for the back bodice. Don't forget the seam and hem allowance.

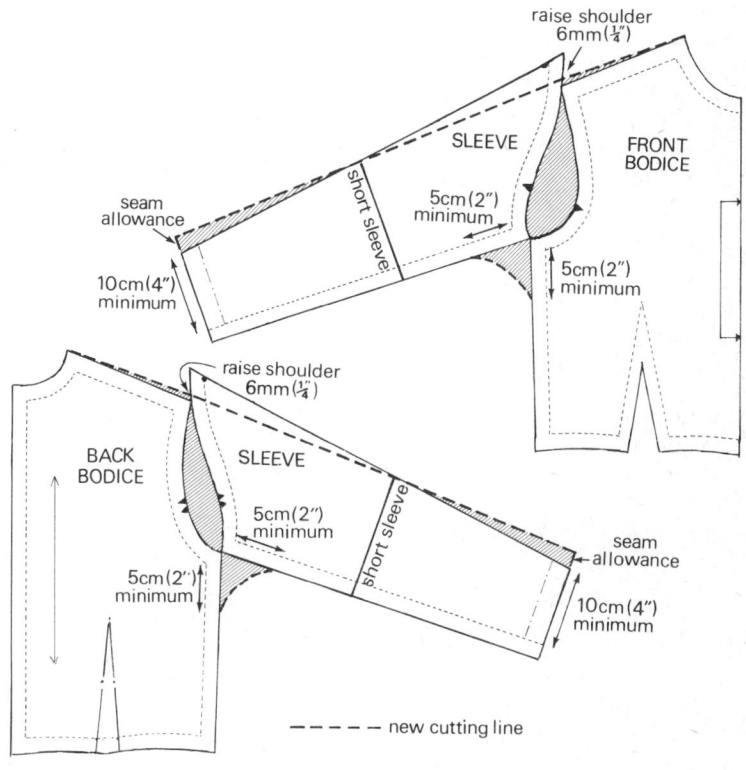

Figure 22

Phase 3

Preparing your fabric and cutting out

Most materials are constructed of vertical and horizontal threads woven regularly under and over each other, see Figure 23. The vertical threads run parallel with the finished edge of your fabric which is called the SELVEDGE. Your garment will have a lop-sided hang to it if these vertical threads do not hang straight down your body.

All paper pattern pieces have straight lines with arrow heads printed on them at each end. These are called GRAIN marks. When you pin your pattern pieces on to the fabric, these arrows must lie exactly parallel with the fabric selvedge. This is called cutting on the STRAIGHT GRAIN. This also applies to garments or parts of garments cut on the BIAS or CROSS GRAIN, when the arrows will be marked diagonally across the pattern piece. Cutting a garment on the bias gives greater stretch to the fabric, but creates problems of drooping hems and shapeless skirts after wearing.

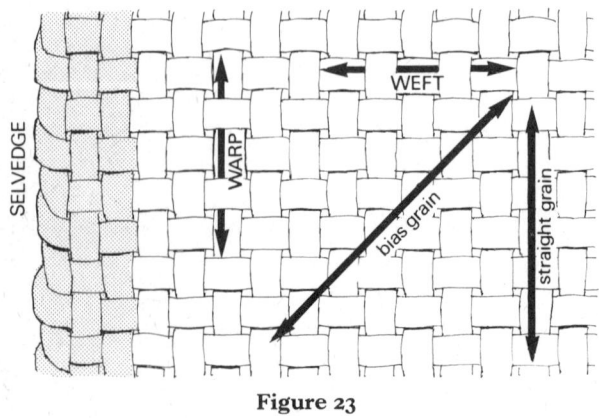

Figure 23

Before you cut out

Laying on the pattern pieces correctly is a crucial part of dressmaking and you cannot be too careful in your preparation. If a wrongly placed piece is cut out it could ruin the whole garment and mean wasted effort and money. The following points should be studied closely as they are designed to prevent irrevocable errors.

1 Check your fabric. Open out the entire fabric length and check for flaws in the weave, misprinting or marks. Unless the length was sold to you as being faulty, do return it to the shop and exchange it for a perfect length if you are not satisfied.

2 Does your fabric have a distinct 'up' or 'down' pattern? Find out which way the design goes and lightly chalk direction arrows on the *wrong* side of your fabric.

3 Like one-way patterned fabrics, velvet and pile fabrics also have a correct up or down direction. Most dressmakers prefer to sew their garment with the pile brushed upwards, towards the face, giving the fabric a darker, richer colour. This does have the disadvantage of being less durable than brushing the pile downwards to the hem. It is a question of personal choice and the style and colour of the pile fabric to be used. Whichever way you choose, remember to chalk the arrows as before and lay all the pattern pieces facing the same direction, otherwise you will end up with a strange, two-toned outfit!

4 Checked and striped materials require careful thought and preparation before cutting out. There is a special section on techniques for these fabrics at the end of this phase.

5 Lightly press the length if necessary. Deep creases can add surplus to your garment in surprising places.

6 Some materials need to be shrunk before you begin to cut out your garment. This process applies particularly to pure wool fabrics. Gently press the length of fabric between two moist pressing cloths with a warm iron. The steam generated by the heat and moisture will shrink the wool fibres.

7 Clear enough floor or table space to lay out the length of fabric.

8 Fold your fabric according to given pattern instructions, laying the right side of your fabric *inside* the fold. This will make it easier to transfer pattern marks later on and also protect the fabric surface.

9 It is important to check that the selvedge is straight and exact and that the fold of the fabric is flat and unwrinkled. Pattern pieces marked to be cut on the fold must be placed *exactly* on the fold. Inaccuracy will result in unwanted surplus in your garment. Use the selvedge edge wherever possible as a seam edge—it saves finishing the raw edge later.

10 Lay the pattern pieces on to the fabric following your pattern layout chart. Pin each pattern corner on to the fabric. You will find too many pins make extra work and possibly mark your fabric. Try to use the long pins recommended in the equipment list, the extra length and fine shaft of the pin will hold the material better. You will find it easier to put the pins in to the material at right angles to the cutting edge of the pattern.

Check

Before you take your scissors to the fabric:
1 Have you laid out all the pattern pieces required for the style?
2 Are the grain lines straight?
3 Have you the correct number of collars, pockets, hoods or facings? (The pattern will tell you to cut 2 or cut 4 etc.)
4 Have you remembered to lay all the pattern pieces one way on directional fabric?

Cut out

Don't be frightened! Take strong, confident cuts into the fabric. Don't let your inexperience or the expense of the fabric inhibit you. If you find the floor is too uncomfortable at this stage, roughtly cut out the pattern shapes on the floor and complete the cutting and marking process on a table. Your careful preparations are now taking shape in front of you, so enjoy watching this exciting happening.

Checked and striped fabrics

Checked and striped materials present their own problems of matching. These can be avoided by careful thought and preparation before cutting out. If you follow these guidelines you should not go wrong.

1 Study the design of the garment you plan to make and decide which colour stripe will look best down the centre of the garment, or which line of check will lie best on the hem. Mark these positions

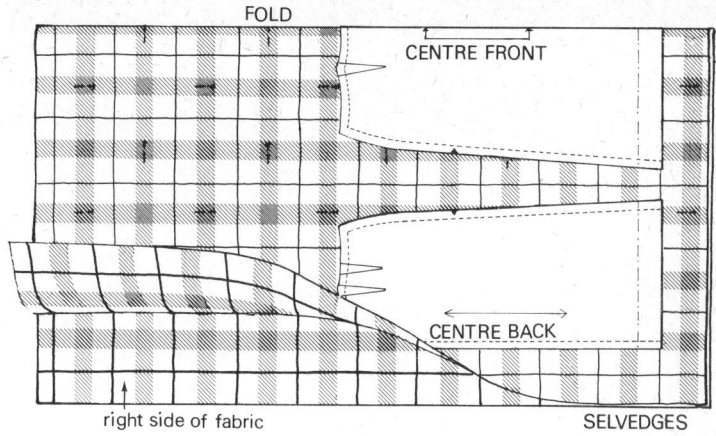

FOLD

CENTRE FRONT

CENTRE BACK

right side of fabric   SELVEDGES

Figure 24

of stripe or check lightly on your pattern pieces at the back, front and side seams. This will simplify pattern matching when pinning pattern pieces on to your fabric.

2 Fold the material as your pattern layout suggests. Remember that the right side of the fabric should be *inside* the fold.

3 Roll the top layer of the folded fabric back to the fold line and pin the lines of check or stripe exactly on top of each other. Continue rolling forward the top layer and pinning *accurately* at approximately 30 cm (12 in) intervals down and across the fabric, as shown in Figure 24.

4 Lay the pattern pieces on to the pinned fabric according to the pattern layout, taking care to match the positions of check or stripe as already marked on the pattern pieces.

5 Always run through the check-list on p. 37 before cutting out. If some of the pins hinder the scissor blades, you can carefully ease the offending pin out whilst cutting.

Phase 4

Preparing to sew

Paper pattern pieces are printed with a great deal of information to help you make up your garment accurately. There are various methods of transferring this information from the pattern piece to the fabric underneath. Which of these methods you use depends on your sewing temperament. Some people enjoy the gentle relaxation of hand sewing, while others prefer, or need, speed. So experiment, and find the approach that suits you. As your dressmaking confidence grows you will find you will need fewer of the balance and identification marks to help you.

Transferring markings

TAILOR'S TACKS (Figure 25)

These are especially good for patient hand sewers. Make two loose stitches, one on top of the other, through the layers of fabric and paper pattern. When all the marks are sewn, gently remove the

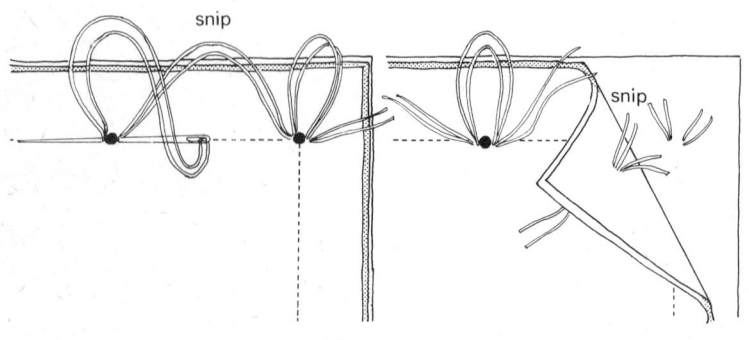

Figure 25

40

paper pattern. Ease the fabric apart and snip the loop to leave tufts of thread on each side, on the right side of the fabric. This method can tear your paper pattern and delay progress when removing threads after machining the seam.

CARBON PAPER AND TRACING WHEEL (Figure 26)

A quick, accurate method for all transfer marking, this is especially good for beginner dressmakers who wish to mark all seam lines and corners to aid their machine stitching. The more proficient dressmaker won't find this necessary as her eye is accustomed to judging the width of seam from the fabric edge. Fold the carbon paper in half with the darker side *inwards*. Slip the folded carbon over the two layers of fabric so that the carbon will mark the wrong side of the fabric when you run the serrated wheel along the lines you wish to transfer. Press hard on the wheel to make clear markings. Beware—the wheel can also tear paper patterns if used roughly. This method is not good for very light and sheer fabrics.

SCISSOR SNIPS (Figure 27)

Another quick method for transferring balance and identification marks is to make small scissor snips within the seam allowance where needed. These snips are easy to see and feel during the sewing of the garment but disappear when the garment is turned out to the right side. You should keep to a constant rule for easy identification—two snips for back pieces and one for the front.

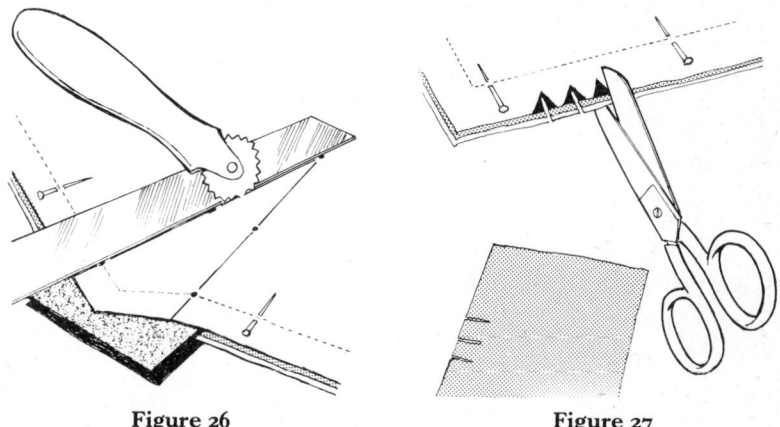

Figure 26   **Figure 27**

PIN AND CHALK (Figure 28)

An ultra quick method is a combination of pin and chalk and scissor snips which will cover the pattern marking requirements of the confident dressmaker. After snipping balance marks, as in Figure 27, pierce with a pin the end of the dart or whatever point is required. Roll the paper pattern carefully back and chalk the pin mark. Turn the fabric over and chalk the pin mark on the other side.

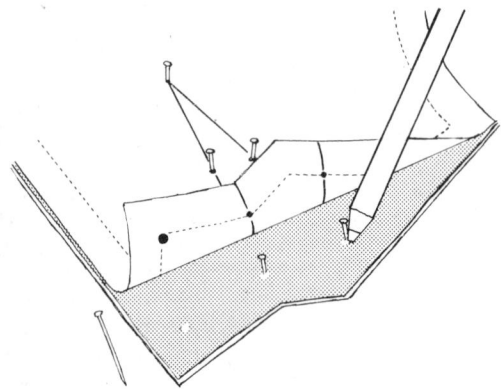

Figure 28

Body measurement chart

	metric	imperial
1 Bust		
2 Waist		
3 Hips		
4 Bust point		
5 Front neck to waist		
6 Front neck to hem		
7 Front waist to hem		
8 Shoulder		
9 Upper arm		
10 Under arm		
11 Top arm		
12 Wrist		
13 Across back		
14 Back neck to waist		
15 Back neck to hem		

Useful personal measurements

	metric	imperial
Dress length (shoulder to hem)		
Dress length (shoulder to floor)		
Skirt length (waist to hem)		
Short sleeve length		
Long sleeve length		
Blouse length (shoulder to waist or hip)		

Approximate yardages for bargain buys

fabric width	dress, long sleeves	skirt	blouse, long sleeves
90 cm (36 in)			
115 cm (45 in)			
150 cm (60 in)